Dedicated to Every Aamchi Local Commuter

Past, Present and Future

AAMCHI LOCAL

Real experiences of a
'Khattar Localkar'

MURALEEDHARAN
APPATH

Made with ❤ on the Notion Press Platform
www.notionpress.com

Contents

Monday

Irresistible Call

"Railways is your property"

Two men seated on Platform No.1 of Borivali Railway Station appear to be free from the usual hustle of daily commutes. Yet, for some unknown reason, they are here; idling oldies?- hard to say. Surprisingly, their expressions exude a sense of pride as if simply being on the platform is an accomplishment! They seem to revel in this moment of aimless leisure. Oddly, there is a palpable sense of 'ownership' in their demeanour, as though the entire platform and the local trains are somehow theirs. Perhaps, the constant announcement ***"railways is your property"*** has taken on a deeper meaning for them! Whatever the case, they appear to be the self-appointed "lords of all they survey" on the platform, free from the fear of anyone asking them to leave.

In a prayerful connection?

Curiously, their heads and spines are held straight and erect - not slumped down or leaning forward - which suggests they are neither dozing off nor distracted. They remain silent, in an alert posture with their eyes gently closed most of the time.

Place of no disturbance?

Nobody on the platform pays any attention to them. Even if they were to sit here all day, undisturbed, no one would mind!. The people bustling about are engrossed in their own lives, too busy to concern themselves with others, the hallmark of Mumbai's fast-paced lifestyle, mirrored here on the platform.

What purpose?

But what are these two gentlemen doing on a busy Mumbai platform, during the morning rush, and on a working day, no less?. Have they come to crowd the station unnecessarily?. Or have they been cast out of their homes?. Let's find out:

Who are they?

These two are Aravi and Bala, old friends and retired senior citizens. Aravi lives in Yogi Nagar, Borivali west, while Bala resides in Alica Nagar, Kandivali east.

Morning mission

During their working years, Mumbai local trains were like a 'second home' to them. A significant part of their lives was spent riding the 'locals' and navigating the platforms. Rushing to embrace the charm, energy, speed and punctuality of the 'locals' was the first thing for them every working day morning. Catching the 7.43am train was a ritual, often involving a daring & risky jump to reach the prized window seat first. Within minutes, compartments would overflow with commuters, leaving only the roof unoccupied! The journey would then begin with the resounding chorus of ***'Ganapati Bappa Morya'*** from all the passengers.

Localkar, Khattar Localkar

Inside the crowded compartments, a unique culture thrived - regulars, strangers, and friends together in laughter, arguments, games of cards, reading newspapers, singing bhajans, celebrating festivals and birthdays, with immense energy & joy, all in a few square feet of shared space!; what to say about the mirth, taunts, short naps, sarcasm, silly quarrels sometimes leading to fights.

Vada-pav sessions with casual chats carried on, completely indifferent to the sweltering heat and stifling humidity inside the coach. Backpacks, shoulder bags, and briefcases dangled from every available space, while no one flinched ***even when their physical bodies were encroached upon*** - all for the shared goal of reaching their workplaces on time. This distinctive travel culture, embraced by every local commuter - '***Localkar, Khattar Localkar***' - is deeply ingrained in the veins of these two old friends, now seen leisurely idling here.

Alas! Then came retirement, abruptly bringing an end to those action-packed, thrilling days.

Change in routine

Initially, like many retirees, they slept long in the mornings, free from alarm clocks. Over time, they focused on financial planning, family duties, and trips to places they had missed earlier, including pilgrimages.

Call of 'local'

However, through it all, they felt the absence of the 'local' - its energy, vibrations, and unspoken camaraderie. They hoped this longing would fade with time, but on the contrary, it only grew stronger as the days passed by. Eventually, the ***'call of the locals'*** became so irresistible that they are back here now with a vengeance to reconnect with their past commuting days!

They are here with valid tickets, though they don't travel much anymore - only a few days a month. Age has tempered all their activities to a large extent.

However, they've committed to coming daily this week to this platform, from Monday to Sunday, as a special case. This is to reflect 0n the humorous & enlightening experiences they gained during their local commutes - memories that shaped their lives over the years.

Like a shy lover approaching her beloved, softly and silently, a 'local' majestically arrives at the platform and aligns with it beautifully!.

"We wouldn't have survived in Mumbai without this 'local', ***a wonder on wheels'***. Bala broke the silence.

"Yes, of course. We owe our lives to this urban miracle. It is ***our Goddess"***. Aravi agreed.

“Today I can’t stay for long because I need to visit the State bank to submit my Life Certificate. It’s November, you know. I went yesterday, but server issues delayed the work”. Bala excused.

“It’s ok. We will meet tomorrow then.”

Tuesday

God in disguise

Like yesterday, they are here on the platform, seated in a seemingly meditative posture. It seems they share a deep emotional connection, something akin to a ***yoga-like union*** with their ***manifest Goddess,*** the '***lifeline of Mumbai,***' undistracted by anything else.

There are only a few commuters on the platform now, perhaps because a train has just left the station. Nothing to worry about - within minutes, the platform will be bustling again, with people rushing in from everywhere!

A little help

A blind person (differently abled) is searching for something with the help of his walking stick. Bala noticed this and got up.

'Kya dhundte ho?' ('What are you looking for?.') Bala asked.

'Ithar do rupee ka paani shop kute?' ('Where is the Rs. 2/- water shop?.') the man enquired.

Bala led him to the Water Vending Machine and helped him get water.

'Ghar se paani saath me kyon nahi lete?' ('Why don't you carry water from home?.') Bala joked in a lighter vein.

'Main roj lata hoon saab. Aaj bhool gaya.' ('I carry it every day, sir. But today, I forgot.') A good reply.

'Ab kidhar jaana hai?' ('Where do you need to go now?.') Bala asked.

'Divyangajan ka dabba pe chod do. Ithar left mein hai.' ('Leave me at the coach for the differently abled. It's on the left side.') Though blind, he knew exactly where his coach was!

Bala helped him board the coach meant for the differently abled.

Doors open to all

Whatever the handicap, 'locals and platforms' are open to everyone. Able-bodied or otherwise, they welcome all. Scores of differently abled people travel every day to work or workshops on the locals. This includes women too. They all reach their destinations safely and return home the same way. In case of any difficulty, just show it, and a helping hand will rise from somewhere. No problem!

"Yesterday, we were talking about our survival in Mumbai, which we owe to the 'locals.' Correct?." Bala said, stirring up nostalgia.

Helplessness in early years

"Yes, yaar. Back in the late 1970s, when we had no money for even one meal a day, forget about going anywhere, traveling was a must to attend job interviews. With no money, road travel by bus or rickshaw was impossible. The only option left was the local trains," Aravi recalled.

"Our curse was that we had university degrees and were looking for white-collar jobs!"

Planning for travel without ticket

"When we were stuck like that, not knowing what to do, you remember, our common friend Joseph came up with the idea of traveling on the locals without a ticket. He'd already been doing it for some time then," Aravi said, taking a deep breath.

Ticketless travel is a chronic issue for Mumbai locals. There are various reasons for this: long queues at ticket counters, lack of time, lack of money, or in rare cases, an unwillingness to spend money on tickets.

Training for travel without ticket

"Left with no other option, we all agreed to try our luck. Joseph skillfully trained us in how to trick TCs, how to escape their eyes. It was like a game of 'cat and mouse' or 'hide and seek.' I remember, he told us to walk confidently, never showing fear or suspicion on the face, because TCs are adept at reading body language. He used to say, 'Don't bother about looking for TCs, and they won't notice you that way. ***Don't fret about the crowds - they're in fact a blessing - a God sent one - for the people like us to survive here.*** Stick with them, move with them. They'll protect you from all sides.' It worked really well for all of us till we finally got some money to buy monthly passes. That's how we survived, thanks entirely to the **blessings of the locals."** Aravi paused for a moment.

"Now we understand that traveling without a valid ticket is a punishable offense. And it was wrong on our part to do so at any time or in any situation. However, back then, it was a case of '***ignorance is bliss,***' combined with helplessness and the strong desire to survive. It is said that when we pray to God in extreme difficulties, He helps us by disguising as friends or situations. And in our case, ***God appeared***

as Amchi locals and the crowds! " Aravi said, pausing briefly.

Blunder of a lifetime

"But I made a terrible blunder one day, you know."

"At that time, I was working at Masjid. One day, my boss sent me to the GPO (General Post Office) at CSMT (then VT) to send some parcels urgently. Being a private company, there was no reimbursement for conveyance expenses. You simply did what they asked you to do. Salary? It could come on the 5th, 10th, or even 15th of next month".

"For the onward journey to CST, I was lucky. However, on the return journey, my training failed me, and a TC caught me at Masjid, mainly because the platform was nearly empty. When TC asked for my ticket, I grew nervous and began frantically pretending to search - patting down my shirt and pant pockets, rummaging through my wallet - everywhere. The TC, sensing my act, stood very close to me, ready to grab me by the collar any time."

"I thought of everything in a flash in those microseconds : losing my first job which I got after many failed attempts at different places, the groceries you all were waiting for me to buy with the money the company promised to pay me that day, the ultimatum you gave me to either pay or vacate the room in Ulhasnagar & return to native place, and the prayers of my parents & siblings back in native place, who expected me to succeed here in the 'city of dreams' and to receive monthly 'Money Orders' afterwards".

"With no money and a hungry stomach, sheer desperation took over me. I felt giddy, furious and what not!. My life and all my dreams were teetering on the brink of collapse as the TC stood before me, poised to act at any moment. At that moment, an overwhelming survival instinct surged within me like a powerful wave. Under its compelling force, I instinctively pushed the TC aside, and moving with lightning speed, I scaled the long stairs, taking four to five steps at a time, dashed past the ticket booking counter area, crossed the long railway bridge, and in mere seconds, found myself on the busy public road at the east side of Masjid station, at CSMT end, like an arrow streaking through the wild!"

"The TC loudly shouted, 'Pakdo, pakdo!' ('catch him, catch him'), and ran behind me for some distance. Then, I was running for life but TC.........! Luckily, no one caught me, and there were no RPF personnel also around. It was a providential escape." Bala concluded.

"Had you been caught, your life would have taken a different turn," Aravi wondered.

"True. lock-up, court case, fine—who knows where it might have led?". Bala admitted.

"Good you escaped, or you might have fallen into the underworld's net. Those were the days of recruitment for underworld kings, like Haji Masthan, Karim Lala, Varadarajan Mudaliar, and the like." Aravi added.

Positives of lapses

"Sometimes, lapses in the systems of controls, checks & balances, serve a good purpose. After all, ***'the end justifies the means'.*** I'm sure someone is still trying what we once did, and the locals might still smile at such pranks." Bala said.

"But, you never told me about this before!" Aravi made his discontent clear.

"I was scared of the authorities. Hence, never disclosed to anyone so far". Bala replied.

"But railways can still take action against you, if they want to". Aravi tried to frighten Bala.

Value of a ticket

"You're always asking me why I'm taking tickets to CSMT, Churchgate, Virar, etc. even when I'm not travelling. You see, tickets are a feeling for me. I just keep them in my pocket for some time. It comforts me quite a lot. After all, ***who knows its value more than me".*** Bala said with a sense of debt and gratitude.

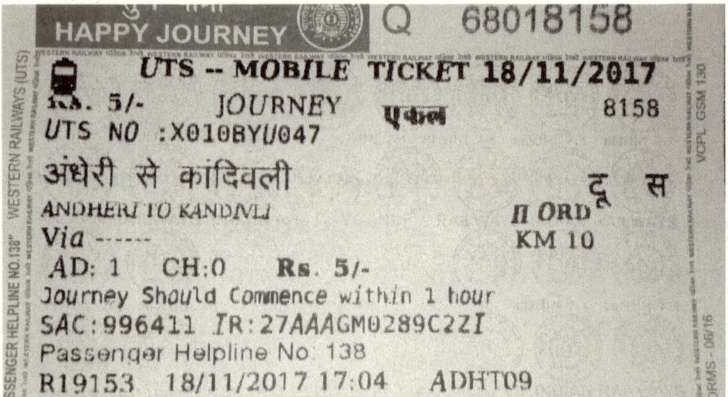

HAPPY JOURNEY Q 68018158
UTS -- MOBILE TICKET 18/11/2017
RS. 5/- JOURNEY एकल 8158
UTS NO :X010BYU047
अंधेरी से कांदिवली दू स
ANDHERI TO KANDIVLI II ORD
Via ------ KM 10
AD: 1 CH:0 Rs. 5/-
Journey Should Commence within 1 hour
SAC:996411 IR:27AAAGM0289C2ZI
Passenger Helpline No: 138
R19153 18/11/2017 17:04 ADHT09

"You're sounding crazy," Aravi laughed.

“That’s okay. But, I think, in addition to transit, there is a unique civilization in locals and the stations surrounding them.” Bala started thinking aloud.

“Well, let’s talk more tomorrow.” Aravi said.

Wednesday

Unity in Diversity

Aravi has already reached the platform. He is now waiting for his friend. Perhaps Bala got stuck in traffic.

It is the end of ***November - winter magic in Mumbai.*** The weather is very pleasant, an ideal time to hang around. It will stay like this for a couple of months or so.

Borivali platforms 1 & 2

Sitting on Borivali platforms 1 and 2 is a delightful experience. These platforms are quite spacious, with a clear east-side view and a gentle breeze blowing most of the time.

The time is around 11.30am in the morning. Since peak hours are over, there is less crowd now.

The sun is shining above in all its glory, and in its light, about a dozen railway tracks below appear as long silver streaks stretching far beyond!.

There are many pillars on these platforms. Around them, a neat arrangement of granite seating allows three or four people to sit comfortably under each setup. Additionally, a few steel benches are provided for waiting commuters.

An overhead fan rotates lazily a few feet away from Aravi. Though it isn't producing much airflow in its fatigued state, thankfully, it's not noisy either.

Bala arrived now.

"Why are you late? Traffic?" Aravi enquired.

Road travel v/s train travel

"Yes. Traffic as usual. The distance from my residence to Kandivali railway station is about 3 km by road, but traffic is unpredictable. Sometimes it takes 10 minutes, sometimes 20, 30, or even an hour or more. When traffic doesn't move at all, I get out of the rickshaw and walk."

"From Churchgate to Kandivali, about 35 km, I can reach in an hour with a fare of ₹15 by local train. But from there to my residence, the shared rickshaw fare is ₹20, and the time taken is 'anytime.'" Bala said upsettingly..

"See how affordable, reliable, and speedy our locals are. They are indeed ***'the lifeline of Mumbai,"*** Aravi said joyously.

Oneness inside the coaches

"Look inside the coach; it's fascinating. ***It's a 'mini-India' in motion.*** People from the north and south, east and west; educated and uneducated; students and teachers; working and retired; young and old; healthy and sick; doctors and patients; employed and unemployed; rich and poor; theists and atheists; tall and short; hungry and not hungry; those with homes and the homeless; married and unmarried; silent and talkative; soft and loud talkers; well-dressed and otherwise; clean and unclean; shaven and unshaven; handsome and otherwise; urban and rural; from high rises, low rises, chawls and slums; new to the city and otherwise; all religions and no religion; homosexuals, bisexuals, transgenders, and more….

Nair, Iyer, Menon, Memon, Chettiyar, Mudaliyar, Salian, Rao, Rai, Bangera, Bhageria, Bangar, Pawar, Sawant, Patel, Patil, Ahuja, Sinha, Singh, Bhuller, Pathak, Gala, George, Khan, and more...all together in this very little space of a coach, speaking different languages, with different food habits, different styles, different purposes...In short, a diverse spectrum of humanity, encompassing various socio-economic, cultural, religious, and educational backgrounds - ***a vibrant blend of it all... ...Where else on Earth can one find such a diverse gathering with cross purposes for a short time in a small moving space like this?"***

"And they coexist, adapting to one another in cramped conditions, often taking awkward physical postures—balancing on one leg due to lack of space for the other; stretching an arm uncomfortably to grab a distant handle, sometimes stretching over a shorter person's head, ending up with his face under someone's armpit to his dismay; enduring relentless nudges from an obese passenger behind, and so on".

"Yet, no one complains. Ignoring extreme discomfort, everyone shares the space to travel to their destinations. Regular commuters even go further; they form bonds, make lasting friendships, attend family functions, help one another with jobs or marriage proposals, and so on. This travel group easily becomes their extended family members too."

Creator to be proud of?

"I believe the Creator should present this 'local life' as a shining example of harmonious human coexistence and mutual accommodation. In a world plagued by conflicts - both globally and within our own country - due to the absence of such harmony, this coexistence, though for a short duration, serves as a beacon of hope." Aravi looked upward with a prayerful expression."

"***And this is a matter of great pride for all the local commuters***. It also shows the astounding level of inner maturity and growth achieved by them, that too without any sophisticated coaching or formal training." Bala added.

Civilization on its banks?

"This culture even extends to the areas surrounding suburban railway stations. Everything is available near the stations at competitive prices and with plenty of options. Time-starved Mumbaikars can quickly buy whatever they need in the station vicinity. Daily travel and daily purchases go hand in hand for them . This ecosystem, cultivated and nurtured by the locals, breathes convenience and efficiency into travelers' everyday lives."

"One day, our trains were delayed in the evening due to some technical problems. I somehow squeezed into the first train that came to Dadar. I reached Kandivali around 9.30pm and headed straight to the 'bhaji market' in the west, as usual".

"The market was enveloped in gloom. Every vendor was worried. Without trains running, no one visited the market. How would they sell their perishable items now? It was nearing 10.00pm. Many vendors had taken loans from moneylenders in the morning at high interest, promising to repay by night. If they couldn't repay the loan with interest, there would be compound interest the next day, no subsequent loans, and a hit to their creditworthiness too.

"Tea stalls, vada-pav & samosa joints, hotels, restaurants, permit rooms, bars, juice vendors, roadside sellers of readymade dresses, chappals, toys, etc., - all were without work, anxiously asking, 'What happened to the locals?' Even the homeless, who had made the surrounding areas of railway stations their homes, were concerned. Call girls were also desperate. The streets were deserted. Autos and buses were waiting for passengers. The losses were immense, and some people went to bed on empty stomachs. ***Where else on Earth can you find such an impact on so many lives due to a few hours of disruption in services***?" Bala concluded emotionally.

"Oh, what a cascading effect. I never realized its magnitude before. Truly, the civilization around stations relies on the locals for sustenance. ***In earlier***

civilizations, no rivers meant no life around. Now, no locals, no life around!" Aravi remarked.

"No doubt. I agree. But you also spoke about gays and transgenders. Have you encountered them in the locals?" Bala asked.

"Yes. It's a secret. I'll tell you tomorrow." Aravi replied.

Thursday

Sexual Orientations

"I didn't have anything in the morning. Let's go and eat something," Bala suggested.

"Okay, we'll go to the Railway Cafeteria on platform No.10. It's very good, with a variety of items at reasonable rates," Aravi said.

"But we have to walk a lot," Bala cautioned.

Escalators & Lifts for all?

"Walk we must, especially at this age. Walk slowly, looking around, feeling the vibrancy of the 'platform energy.' Don't worry about climbing stairs like in earlier days. Escalators and lifts are in operation these days. If the escalator is not comfortable, we can take a lift. You see, lifts are meant for 'Divyangajan' and seniors like us. This is prominently written and displayed at the entrance itself. But here's the catch: who reads and who bothers? Policing these things is not practical for Railways. Hence, lifts are mostly used by able-bodied & youngsters - a very lazy lot, today's millennials and Gen Z! In the worst case, we may have to wait there for a while. That's all."

Free Deckside View

"See the concourse on the first level - very wide, less crowded, airy, with a beautiful upper-deck view. We can sit here and relax for hours together; no rent, no electricity charges, no calling bell, no visitors, no household chores, no boss or servant, and no need for adherence or conformity to anything. Absolute freedom. Heaven on earth, isn't it?"

Borivali–what does it lack?"

"About a kilometer to the east from here is the National Park with thick forests, mountains, valleys, rivers, wild animals, and curiously, many ancient

(Kanheri) caves made in hard rock ***where monks once meditated on the miracle and purpose of life***. A few kilometers to the west (Gorai and Aksa) or north (Bhayandar) is the Arabian Sea with backwaters. And between these two is Borivali, with all modern facilities and a cosmopolitan-type population. Food, very important - don't worry - every type is available round the clock. No issue. ***Where else on earth, in a few square kilometers, can we see such a place with mountains, valleys, wild animals, rock caves on one side, and the deep sea & related activities on the other, sandwiched between them lakhs of cosmopolitan people with endless varieties of food and other items 24/7?***" Aravi wondered.

"That way, Mumbai is a blessed city, with moderate weather and all of nature's bounties. Everything, everything, **except snowfall!** Due to climate change, that too we can expect in due course," Bala added, and both laughed for a while.

"Okay, now come to 'local' life. Let's not digress too much," Bala redirected.

Health benefits - local travel

"Earlier, if traveling by 'local,' there was no need for other exercises. The needed exercise was integrated into the '***local lifestyle***' : brisk walk from residence to the bus stop or rickshaw stand, as the case may be, and from there to railway station, often swaying both ways to avoid being hit by others coming in the opposite direction, jumping over a manhole or a dug-up road, abruptly stopping to make way for rushing people - all this is aerobics, correct? Further, climbing stairs, running to catch the incoming train, and pushing oneself into the coach - if these aren't exercises, then what are they? Then comes steam therapy with continuous perspiration expelling all the toxins! ***Everything with no extra burden of time or money!"***

Comforts at the Cost of Health?

"Now, pick up & drop facilities, Escalators, AC trains and many other conveniences provide comfort in every way. But sadly, all of these take a toll on our health too in all ways; new and ever-evolving germs and lifestyle diseases. What a tragedy!" Aravi said and continued.

'Local body odour?'

"An interesting thing is coming to my mind in this context. Some people, mainly from the middle class, get up very early in the morning, go for a walk and other exercises, come home, take a bath, apply deodorants, body sprays, etc. and go to the office clean and fresh. My boss was such a one."

"Whereas in my case, I traveled by 'local.' My body odor was a mix of my sweat and others' in the 'local.' My office was centrally air-conditioned, and all my sweat would dry quickly and stick to my body, producing a peculiar **'local odor."**

"My boss would call me to his cabin, ask me to sit near him, and work on the PC. My body odor would then make him irritable, and he would always expel the outgoing breath through his nose forcefully, making a certain noise like a hissing cobra! He was incredibly polite and never showed this to me, and unfortunately, I wasn't able to assist him either. But then, he summoned me to his cabin only when it was absolutely necessary. In a way, the locals helped me avoid my boss as well! Looking back, it feels quite amusing," Aravi remarked with a chuckle.

"Really funny. You said something about homosexuals and transgenders yesterday?" Bala asked.

Weird experience

"Yes, I know you're curious. It was in the early 1990s. I was staying in Dombivli at that time. You know how crowded and chaotic it gets there. As usual, I managed to squeeze into a fast local train. It was extremely packed - only two or three of us could get in. I was stuck in the main passage near the entrance, with no room to move further inside. The train only stopped at Thane and Ghatkopar before reaching my destination, Dadar. The platform at Thane was on the opposite side, while at Ghatkopar, it was on my side. So, I turned toward the door, ready to manage the crowd that would rush in at Ghatkopar."

"After the train left Thane, those planning to alight at Ghatkopar began moving toward my side. It was unbearably crowded, stiflingly hot, and the fans weren't working. Everyone was sweating profusely."

"That's when I felt something odd at my lower back - some movement, some rubbing. The person behind me was tall, handsome, and looked quite decent. At first, I couldn't make sense of it, but then I realized he was trying to ***thrust his 'stick' against me.*** Failing to find an opening, he kept it moving around my lower back. That's when I remembered something my friend Joseph had once told me. I understood what was happening but couldn't move an inch, let alone resist or turn around. The man leaned heavily against me like a buffalo, though his hands were raised above."

"In frustration, I said, 'Barabar khade ho jana. Aap itna hilta kyun? Aap mere upar kyun girte ho?' ('Stand properly. Why are you moving so much? Why are you leaning on me?'}

"He replied, 'Barabar to hoon…aapko kya takleef? Gadi mein naya kya? Gaadi mein aisa hi hota hai.' ('I'm standing properly. What's your problem? Are you new to train travel? This is how it is in trains'). Saying this, he leaned back slightly with his upper body but continued his ***'mission'*** below."

"My hands were clutching the overhead bars for support. With great effort, I freed one hand, reached down, and firmly grabbed his ***'instrument.'*** Fortunately, I had grown nails then, which became my weapon. I twisted and clawed at it with all my strength. The guy couldn't do anything. Unable to bear the pain, his 'stick' started shrinking. Since his zip was open, I could easily follow it to its base, where its ***two 'dangling associates'*** also fell under my grip. I attacked those as well. Only pain for him, ***no 'relief'***—much to my satisfaction."

"As Ghatkopar station approached, the guy realized he was in trouble. He wanted to get off, but my grip held him back. He began whispering apologies in my ear, his face showing intense pain, almost in tears. I didn't want to escalate the matter further as I also was very scared and disturbed a lot, so I let him go.

"After reaching Dadar, I rushed to the urinals near Kohinoor Hotel, thoroughly washed my hands, and went to my Prabhadevi Office. I never told anyone about it until now," Aravi concluded.

"You didn't tell anyone because you didn't want to tarnish the 'local's' reputation. But now you're sharing it publicly," Bala remarked.

"I disagree. The ***reputation of locals isn't tarnished by such incidents;*** these things happen everywhere—in hotels, offices, and so on. Besides, I don't see myself as a victim in the train. Honestly, I'm more intrigued by how ***he could even get aroused in such a situation***. Some people are wired that way—what can we do? But trying such things on people without their consent and in an inappropriate setting is completely unacceptable. That's all," Aravi added.

Transgenders

"What about transgenders?" Bala asked.

"They're often seen during non-peak hours, moving through trains in groups. They clap their hands, bless commuters by touching their heads, and ask for money. It's not begging; ***it's a 'dakshina' for their blessings. They believe their blessings have immense value.*** You can give or not—it's up to you. They don't pester and simply move on."

"They're well-built, impeccably dressed, and wear a lot of makeup. At stations like Bandra, Mahim, and Matunga, they gather on platforms, often under staircases or in isolated spots, where they apply makeup."

"Two weeks ago, I was at Dadar. A group of transgenders boarded the train at Mahim. Among them was a very beautiful, young transgender with striking features and a charming demeanor. Everyone was stealing glances at her, but she paid no attention and continued her activity. When she came to me, I jokingly said, 'Makeup pe bahut kharcha karti ho, phir humse paisa mangta ho?' ('You spend so much on makeup, and then ask us for money?')"

"Surprised by my question, she replied, 'Bhagwan diya hua badan hum achche se rakhte hain saab, usko hum sundar karte hain…jitna ho sake utna…acha na saab?' ('***This body is given by God, and we keep it beautiful as much as possible. Isn't it good, sir?***')"

"What a ***profound response from a transgender person!*** Most people tend to ignore them - out of fear, disdain, or the assumption that they lack education. Yet, her words carried wisdom that many so-called civilized and educated individuals often fail to grasp. I smiled, handed her some money, and others followed my lead. She got off at the next station to continue her work in other coaches." Aravi said.

"She must have impressed you. Hoping to see her again?" Bala teased.

"Admiration, Bala. Nothing more." Aravi said with a laugh.

"That's okay. But I also know the ***local is a great leveller***—no one is high or low inside the coaches. Then what about those who board it with ***inflated egos?***" Bala asked.

"That's for tomorrow!" Aravi said.

Friday

Liberation

Saturdays – no longer half days

"These days, most offices have a five-day work week, so Friday feels like the weekend. Earlier, it was five full days and half-day Saturdays. But what was the use? No extra sleep, the same routine commute—Saturday half-days felt just like any other working day!" Aravi said.

ICF – Is it visually appealing?

"Okay…first, let's try to recollect that ego-busting incident."

"But before that, there's something important. You see, now-a-days, destinations are displayed electronically inside every local train. They're also displayed in front of the trains. Below the destination display in front, there's something very significant written in bold letters—not electronic, just plain. You know what it is?" Aravi asked.

"No?" Bala replied.

"**I C F .** That stands for **Integral Coach Factory**—the indigenous manufacturer of railway coaches," Aravi explained.

"Really? I never noticed it," Bala admitted.

"Me neither, until recently. Last week, I was standing on the Kandivali platform's overbridge, watching the locals pass below. A train was approaching from Churchgate, and I noticed those letters written prominently below the destination display. I was astonished at how I had missed it all these years - ***perhaps because my mind was always preoccupied with focusing on the destination and hurrying to board the train***. Out of curiosity, I asked my wife about this - she's a true 'Mumbaikar, Localkar'- but even she hadn't noticed it. Surprising, isn't it?" Aravi said.

"Very bad indeed- shameful even! We've been commuting in these coaches, practically our second homes, for decades without noticing who made them. Forget about being respectful. We should feel sorry about this. But on the other hand, I think the railways should also include information like this in their regular announcements. These practices, if adopted across sectors, would instill national pride in the minds of our people. ***Contributions from visionaries and our indigenous capabilities should be highlighted—not just through awards only but through audio-visual outreach too.*** It would inspire common people to a great extent," Bala suggested.

Destination Confusion

"True. Now, speaking of destination displays, I recall an interesting episode from when we were new to Mumbai and living in Ulhasnagar No. 3," Aravi said.

"One day, I hurried to the platform and barely managed to board a moving train at Dadar. In my haste, I misread the destination and even got the wrong confirmation from a co-passenger. It was an Asangaon local, not the Ambernath train I needed. By the time I realized this - after Kalyan - it was too late. The train had taken a different route then. I eventually got off at Shahad station and had to walk three kilometers back to our place at Ulhasnagar."

"Those were also the days of ticketless travel," he added with a smile.

"Another time, the platform indicator, the announcements, and the destination display on the train all showed different destinations. Totally confused, I decided not to board."

"That experience made me very cautious. I began confirming and reconfirming destinations. Once, at Dadar, I ran to catch a train amidst the chaos of commuters boarding. I couldn't find anyone to ask about the destination. There was a man sitting inside the train at the window seat, asleep with his hand as a headrest. I shook his hand through the open window (no window grills then) and asked, 'Kaunsi gaadi hai?' ('Which train is this?')."

His reaction? ('Aiyla Teri Aayi chi…bc…. mc…') A torrent of Mumbai's choicest swear words! I was shocked, terrified, knowing not what to do. Meanwhile, someone nearby clarified the destination to me, and I quickly boarded the train. For a while, I kept my face turned away from him, worried the 'gaali dada' might recognize me and unleash more from his weaponry. But nothing of the sort happened for some time. Later, when everything cooled down, I dared to steal a glance at him through the crowd. To my surprise, there he was, peacefully asleep as if nothing had ever happened!"

"***That day, I truly grasped the essence of the 'local spirit.' In the heat of the moment, we may argue or exchange harsh words, but we let it go quickly and steadily move on with our lives without holding grudges towards anyone.***" Aravi concluded.

Feeling of Liberation

"Notwithstanding such experiences, for me, the locals normally offer a unique sense of freedom. Sometimes, I board a different coach to escape familiar faces. It's my 'me time,' a space where I can be completely myself. Whether I sleep, read, laugh, think, smile, sing, dream, write, without causing any nuisance to others, or even just stand quietly, nobody bothers and ***I relish the anonymity factor very much then.*** No judgment, no expectations, no need to look or appear to be in a certain way. ***It's local therapy for me. Where else can you find such a secure space for instant liberation, that too 2 4/7, at a low cost like this?"*** Aravi further added.

Ego Swallowing

"Now, what about that ego-busting incident from our 7.40am Ambernath-CSMT local," Bala asked.

"Ah, our 'rummy' group! Remember how we played cards on a briefcase balanced on our knees? One day, our usual window seat was occupied by a well-dressed gentleman. At Thane, as per the unwritten rule, we began vacating seats for standing commuters. (***'Ambernathvaala utto...doosare ko***

baitane ko do..Those sitting from Ambernath, please give your seats to the standees'}. Everyone did it willingly. But this one man stubbornly refused to do so. Despite repeated requests, he wouldn't budge an inch. He failed to see reason, and on the contrary, started arguing vehemently. We all got very frustrated and angry at him. Finally, left with no other option, our friend, Khan, physically lifted him off the seat like a small toy and the standees there quickly occupied his seat."

"He was furious, trembling with anger, and started shouting, 'Who do you think you are? RPF or ticket checkers? I'll teach you a lesson. Playing cards is illegal!"

"Despite his rant, we kept our cool. But when he went on about 'teaching us a lesson' and 'how we didn't 'know who he was,' we decided to teach him some of our train lessons too in a way fit for him. At Ghatkopar, we forcibly made him get off the train, even though his destination was CSMT. He kept shouting threats from the platform, but we left him there."

"For weeks, we were anxious, wondering if he'd lodge a complaint. But nothing untoward happened.

Then one day, he was back in our coach, smiling and apologizing for his past behavior. He said he'd observed the same seat-sharing practice in other coaches too and realized then how good, civilised and considerate it was. However, ***his ego had blinded him then from appreciating & cooperating with this practice,*** for which he was extremely shameful. It's true - '***when ego leaves, God enters'.*** Thereafter, he became a regular with us for a long time." Aravi said.

"***Life in the locals teaches us: leave your ego and attitude; all are equal here.*** Be good, and you'll get good in return." Bala said.

"Tomorrow, let's recollect some humorous incidents from local life," Aravi said.

"Alright," Bala agreed.

Saturday

Unique stories

Humorous Incidents in Our Local Life..

Amidst Inequalities

"One day, an elderly man was standing near me in the coach. He was in soiled clothes with unkempt hair. After a while, he began scratching himself all over and eventually limited it to his private parts. In the rush, I even doubted if he was scratching me too. Amused, I asked with a smile:

'Kya itna ghasta ho… raat ko chuha kaata kya?' ('Why are you scratching so much? Did a rat bite you last night?)"

"He immediately stopped scratching. But after some time, he put his hand directly inside his pants and started scratching straight. Amused again, I asked him with a smile":

'Kya hua… kuch takleef hai?' ('What happened? Any problem?)"

"'Nahi sahab… do din se snan nahi kiya… paani nahi aaya chaali pe.' ('No, sir. I haven't taken a bath for two days. No water supply in the chawl)."

'Inequalities and disparities coexist here, yet there's no contempt, no ill will, no comparisons, or one-upmanship. Everyone is treated as equals, with camaraderie.' " Aravi paused and continued.

Robber's Return

"Once at King Circle station, a robber snatched a lady commuter's chain and fled. She screamed but couldn't stop him. Later, she told her friends that it wasn't real gold but imitation jewelry".

"But this robber wasn't one to let it go. A few days later, he appeared before her and gave her a tight slap, yelling, 'Mujhe ch**** banathi kya?' ('You fooled me? How dare you?') before disappearing again!" Aravi recounted.

Outsmarting Railway Staff

"Last month, I tricked a railway staff member at a suburban railway station. " Aravi began.

"I was lying down on a granite platform under a pillar near the washroom. A staff member making rounds told me, 'Utto… yeh sone ki jagah nahi hai.' (Get up… this isn't a place to sleep'.)

"I ignored him with my eyes closed. Then he started shaking me with his baton. I gently opened my eyes and said, 'Main senior citizen hoon. Ticket hai mere paas. Tabiyat theek nahi hai, thoda aaram karke jaa raha hoon.' (I'm a senior citizen. I have a ticket. I'm not feeling well, so I'm resting a bit before I leave.)"

"He replied, 'Tabiyat theek nahi hai to ghar ya hospital jao... yahan kyun?' (' If you're unwell, go home or to a hospital. Why are you here?)"

"I calmly said, 'Agar main yahaan marr gaya to tum fasoge. Log bolenge tumne mujhe maar dala. Tumhari naukri chali jaayegi. Ghar mein biwi-bache hain, aur CCTV sab record kar raha hai.' (If I die here, you'll get into trouble. People will say you killed me. You'll lose your job. You have a family, and CCTV is recording everything.)"

"Looking worried, he quickly left," Aravi said with a chuckle.

Romance on Locals

""Are there ever any chances for romance in locals? People often call local travel boring," Bala asked.

"Of course, there are. ***In fact, platforms and locals are fertile grounds for romance,*** though not the film type. Regulars of opposite sexes often exchange glances, use sign language, or admire each other from a distance at their 'usual spots'. If the interest is mutual, things can progres."

"Sometimes, it ends in marriage or relationships. And if someone gets bored, they can always change trains, timings, or even coaches for a fresh start! There are plenty of options available. ***Locals are never boring,*** " Aravi added.

"Our friend Pawar used to go down to Ambernath from Vithalwadi every day just to secure a window seat and enjoy watching young women on the platforms and elsewhere throughout his entire journey to CSMT. '***Who says local travel is boring?*** ' he'd often remark."

TV Coach

"Do you remember our old 'TV coach'? It had a partition with a see - through upper section - gents on one side and ladies on the other. The gents' side was always overcrowded ***for the 'visual treat' it***

offered all the time! That's why it was aptly called the TV Coach." Aravi further added.

Language Class

Many migrants, in their initial days here, didn't know English, Hindi, or Marathi. However, they would gradually learn these languages from locals by keenly listening to conversations & arguments of fellow commuters. In this way, the ***locals often served as informal coaching classes for languages.***

In some cases, when these migrants were asked something, they would simply smile and nod their heads in apparent agreement. For example, if someone near the door asked, 'Dadar me utrega kya?' ('Will you get down at Dadar?'), they would smile and nod their heads. The commuter would then assume they intended to get off. But when Dadar arrived, the migrants wouldn't move, causing trouble for everyone boarding and alighting.

Reserved Senior Citizen Seats

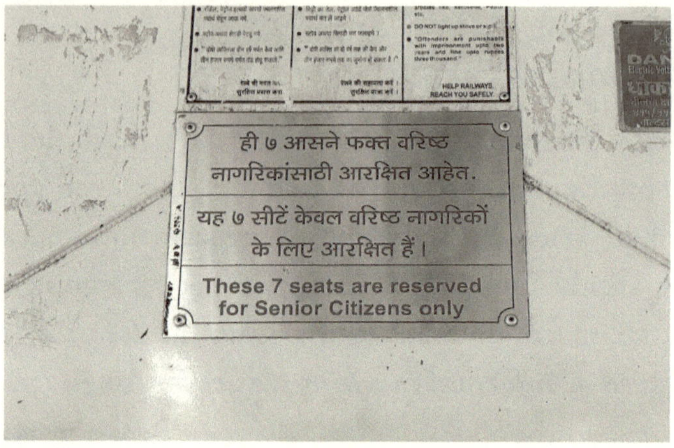

The 7 seats reserved for senior citizens are typically located deep inside the train, in the last row, rather than the first or second rows. Reaching these seats in a crowded train is no easy task, and getting out can be nearly impossible. Often, these seats are occupied by non-seniors. Even if a senior manages to reach them, there's no guarantee of getting a seat. ***It's practically a joke on seniors.***

The Fourth Seat

In earlier days, the seating arrangement in locals was slightly more than enough for three people but not quite enough for four. This allowed a fourth person to partially sit if the other three cooperated. However, not everyone was willing to adjust. If any of the seated individuals were obese, there was no chance at all for the fourth person. Heated arguments would often erupt over this unseen seat:

- 'He bhai, zara sarak na. Thoda baithne do.' ('Please move a little and let me sit'.)
- 'Idhar kidhar jagah hai?' ('Where is space here?')
- 'Aap pair itna phailake kyun baithte ho? Thoda nasdik lao, jagah ho jayegi'. ('Why are you spreading your legs so much? Bring them closer, and there will be space'.)

This seat often left the fourth person in a precarious position: sitting but not quite sitting, falling but not falling, and resting but not resting. To stay seated on the edge, the fourth person would continuously push against the other three in the row, which was exhausting. Eventually, when he ran out of energy, he would rest his head and face wherever it was convenient- ***sometimes in the 'cavity' under the belly of a bulky person standing nearby. In certain cases, this unintended 'private space' became a comforting spot for a quick nap too.*** Such scenes were unique to the locals!

Pole Dance

Newcomers to local trains often create comic scenes. When trains stop at stations, they cling tightly to the central pole near the door, blocking everyone's entry and exit. Frustrated commuters shout, 'He bhai, zara utar ke chado!' ('Please get down first and then board again'), but the newcomers refuse, fearing they won't be able to reboard.

In the resulting chaos, commuters, left with no choice, toss the stubborn passenger around the pole, landing kicks to dislodge him. The individual, however, refuses to let go, bending down to shield his face and offering his back for the kicks instead. It's a sad yet determined scene. Ultimately, the ***newcomer prevails,*** straightening up triumphantly as the train starts, ready to repeat the cycle at the next station.

Sleeping With Mouth Wide Open

An amusing sight in local trains, even during the hot and humid summer days, involves commuters in deep sleep. Despite sitting upright with sweat-drenched shirts, their heads rest against the partition behind, faces turned upward, mouths wide open, snoring, and sometimes with saliva trickling down.

They are completely unaffected by the discomforts around them - ***no need for sleeping pills, cozy beds, or air conditioning. Truly enviable!***

Sleepy Heads

For some commuters, sleep is intermittent. When it arrives, their heads begin swaying like pendulums, inevitably landing on the shoulder of the adjacent person. The latter, who is often awake, becomes irritated, either imagining the disturbance or simply resenting being used as a headrest.

He waits for the next tilt and, just as the head starts to fall, he moves forward, backward, or sideways. The sleepy head, finding no support, drops down with a jerk, startling the sleeper awake. The awakened commuter quickly straightens up as though nothing happened, while the irritated neighbor pretends ignorance, satisfied at having ***'taught a lesson.'*** The cycle repeats endlessly, creating a humorous spectacle unique to the locals.

Boastful Commuters

Some regular commuters use their fixed coaches as platforms to boast about themselves, their company's activities, reputation, and the salaries and perks they enjoy. One such individual frequently bragged about the amount of income tax he supposedly 'paid.' In reality, it was not voluntarily paid by him but deducted by his employer as Tax Deducted at Source (TDS), as he worked for a government organisation. His constant talk was more out of his frustration in his inability to stop paying tax than the pride in paying tax regularly. One day, another passenger humorously asked. ***'Aap kisko paise diya bolte ho?' ('whom did you give money to?') Amusingly, many in the coach didn't even know in those days what income tax was!***

Backpacks or Front Packs - Travel light

Nowadays, commuters often carry large backpacks either slung on their back or placed in front of them. Rarely do they hold these bags in their hands or store them on the overhead racks. For such commuters, this is very convenient because there's no risk of forgetting the bag in the train, and secondly, their hands remain free for uninterrupted mobile use.

However, these bulky bags pose certain problems. ***They take up significant space - sometimes enough***

for an additional passenger - in the already overcrowded local trains. Boarding or alighting becomes even more challenging as these 'packs' block free movement of commuters inside the coach. It's almost as if one commuter with a backpack equals two passengers in terms of space consumption.

In earlier days, most commuters carried small handbags, shoulder bags or sleek briefcases, primarily for their tiffins. While times have changed, and we now carry more items for our convenience, aren't many of them unnecessary?. ***Perhaps, if we chose to 'travel light', the locals could offer more space for everyone.***

Days in Western Railway Quarters, Matunga - A Life Saved By the Local Train

"Do you remember our time in government quarters, like the CPWD Quarters Sahar, CGS Quarters Antop Hill, and the Central and Western Railway Quarters in Matunga?. Allottees in those days would rent out these quarters to us, even though it wasn't authorized to do so. ***It was a tremendous help back then to all of us,*** and without it, we might have ended up on the streets or footpaths."

"At the Western Railway Quarters in Matunga, our friend Venu fell in love with a ***Maharashtrian girl*** who lived nearby. One evening ***her family suddenly came looking for this 'Madrasi'.*** Venu had to run for his life and managed to escape by leaping into a local train that had just started moving at Matunga. Though we were later asked to vacate by the quarter's allottee, the fact that he was saved, thanks to the local train, was a huge relief for us."

"Times have changed for the better. Today's generation is fortunate - they can marry anyone they choose without facing such issues. ***Credit for this goes entirely to advancements in science & technology,*** which have united humanity globally in ways we never imagined back then."

"I wish we had been born in these times." Aravi said with a wistful smile.

Got a Job, Thanks to the Locals!

In the earlier days, local trains had small overhead fans, many of which frequently malfunctioned. Commuters often resorted to using combs to nudge the fan blades through the protective grill, hoping to get them spinning. Sometimes, this quick fix kept the fans running for the entire journey, while other times, it barely worked or failed altogether.

"Do you remember our friend Ramu, who was heading to Masjid for a job interview?"

Back then, Masjid, Princess Street, Kalbadevi, Nagdevi Street and surrounding areas were bustling hubs of opportunity for new migrants. These locations were home to many transport and trading companies that served as stepping stones for many freshers. After gaining some experience, they would often move on to better opportunities elsewhere. Employers in the area were aware of this pattern but still they supported the newcomers wholeheartedly.

"Ramu didn't own a decent shirt for the interview, so Gopi lent him one," Aravi recalled.

As was typical, Ramu boarded a crowded local train. Unable to find a seat, standing in the first lane between rows, he noticed that the overhead fan above him wasn't working. With no chance of relocating in the packed train, he pulled out his comb and tried to spin the fan blades, as many commuters did on such times. To everyone's surprise, the fan roared to life - but it also spewed a cloud of carbon, soot, and dust, showering down on Ramu's head, face, and borrowed shirt.

He was left looking disheveled, with black stains covering him. Still, determined not to miss the interview, he disembarked at Masjid and cleaned himself as best he could. However, the carbon stains remained on his face and shirt as a dry paste.

When he arrived at the interview, the employer couldn't help but smile at his peculiar appearance and asked him what had happened. Ramu honestly explained the incident, describing the malfunctioning fan and his desperate attempt to fix it.

The interviewer, who was also the company's proprietor, was a ***regular first-class commuter and was well-acquainted with such scenarios in local trains.***

Ramu met all the criteria for the job, but ***it was this shared local train experience that created an instant connection with the employer***. That relatability tipped the scales in his favor, and Ramu landed the job!

Free Counseling

"Do you remember our friend Verghese, who always traveled on the footboard, hanging outside while clutching the central pole at the entrance? We warned him countless times, but he never paid heed. He loved the rush of the wind and the view outside. 'Sitting inside the coach is boring,' he'd say.

"One day, just after the Thane tunnel, he started feeling drowsy while still hanging outside. His head drooped a couple of times, and his body slumped slightly, but his firm grip on the pole saved him from a near fall."

"A stranger standing nearby inside the coach noticed this and decided to intervene. Normally, people in the locals avoid interfering, wary of unpleasant reactions. But this stranger took the risk and spoke to Verghese. He effectively counseled him throughout the journey, ensuring Verghese stayed safe until he got down at Dombivli."

"From that day forward, Verghese changed his ways. He stopped standing at the entrance and always moved inside the coach. ***What we couldn't achieve with our prolonged advice, a concerned co-passenger, a complete stranger, managed to***

accomplish in the local in a single day". Aravi recounted.

What a pleasant surprise

In today's digital age, contact details are stored permanently, leaving little chance of losing them any time.

Back in the pre-digital era, things were quite different. People relied on pocket diaries to store contact information, often losing them over time. Consequently, old friends from school or college would lose touch as life took them on different paths.

In those days, the crowded local trains often became the stage for delightful reunions. Friends who hadn't seen each other in years would unexpectedly recognize one another amidst the hustle of finding foot space or during a heated argument. The moment of recognition would spark immense joy and pleasant surprises.

Locals also served as bridges between distant relatives or neighbors from the same panchayats or villages, who became close acquaintances only after crossing paths in the train. Phrases like, ***'Oh, you're***

Gokul's younger brother?' or 'You're from South Kondazhy?' or 'You studied at Ottapalam NSS College? were common and often led to lasting friendships.

During periodical visits to their native places, these newfound connections would also visit each other's homes, carrying customary gifts. ***Local trains didn't just facilitate travel; they helped forge new bonds, rekindle old ties, and strengthen relationships across distances.***

The Coveted Window Seat

The window seat, especially one facing the direction of the train's movement, ***is the best choice seat*** for commuters. Many passengers can't resist the urge to secure it, even before the train comes to a complete stop. Some leap into the coach as it slows down, risking injury by hitting seat edges or slipping, falling and trampling upon others. A certain commuter, spotting a vacant window seat in a nearby row, abandons his current non-window seat and dashes towards it only to lose both seats when a quicker rival claims it first. The resulting look of disappointment on his face is almost comical.

Why all this fuss for the window seat? The window seat offers unparalleled perks - ever-changing scenic views, a refreshing breeze that varies with the train's speed, and a blissful escape from the usual commotion inside the coach. For those traveling to the last stop, it's an unmatched sanctuary of peace.

Picture this: A tiffin bag resting comfortably on your lap, one hand securing it while the other kept on the window for head support. ***You have all the freedom here to gaze outside, ponder life's mysteries, doze off, chat, read, or simply relax. Where else can one find such a seat that delivers pure travel bliss?***

My identity, train's identity?

Earlier, conversations often revolved around one's association with a local train and its schedule. 'Oh, you're on the 7.40 train? Which compartment? I'm in the coach just behind the middle first class,' and so on. Some would even boast, 'My train is the 7:58 double fast' or '8:05 semi-fast,' as if these timings defined a part of their identity.

Regular commuters often formed friendships within their coaches, while others chose to remain reserved, depending on their personalities. Over time, however, the faces of fellow regulars became familiar, creating a silent sense of connection.

This familiarity would prove significant, even surprising, on certain occasions - ***like marriage proposals.*** At family gatherings, two individuals might instantly recognize each other from their train journeys, establishing an immediate rapport between families. The conversation would naturally shift to shared experiences on the local, creating a common ground for discussions. ***The trust and familiarity developed on the train would serve as a foundation for confidence and mutual understanding.***

In the world of locals, once a friend, always a friend—a trusted companion for life!"

Sunday

Sacred Scripture in motion

"Today is Sunday, the day when certain sections of our suburban railway undergo mega blocks. Mumbaikars have grown accustomed to this and now plan their Sunday activities accordingly.

"Since today marks the conclusion of our current session, let's stay a bit longer, have lunch at the railway cafeteria on Platform No. 10, enjoy some evening tea, and then head our separate ways. Sounds good?" Aravi suggested."

Commuters' Responsibility

The digital era has transformed many aspects of life, including human interactions. In locals, this change is particularly noticeable.

Gone are the days of camaraderie and group activities in train coaches. Now, people mostly avoid eye contact, let alone exchanging smiles, handshakes, or greetings - even with long-time co-travelers.

Heads are bent, ears plugged, and eyes glued to mobile screens, motionless except for darting eyeballs and tapping fingers. Occasionally, a phone call interrupts this trance-like state.

This mobile-centric lifestyle is fine as long as commuters remain vigilant. Paying attention to one's own surroundings and items kept on ***overhead racks above one's own head or under the seats of one's own seat - is crucial. Ignoring these could lead to serious consequences,*** as past incidents have already shown. While railways regularly undertake safety measures for our smooth journey, it's also our responsibility to stay alert and support railways in all ways possible.

Escaping Crowds

"When we think of 'local trains,' the first thing that comes to our minds are the huge crowds and the rush. They say you don't even need to make an effort to board - just stand near the coach, and the commuters will do this for you. Similarly, to get off, simply be near the door, and the crowd will do the rest. How do we manage all this?" Bala asked.

"***True. Locals are crowded, often overcrowded, but mostly during peak hours. At other times, it's easily manageable.***

"When it comes to our personal experiences, the truth is that the crowds were of great help during our early days here. They often made it easier for us to evade the TCs. I still remember that one day at Masjid when there was no crowd, and you got caught, didn't you? In a way, the crowds can sometimes be a blessing for certain commuters, wouldn't you agree? Of course, I mean this in a lighter vein".

"In reality, the crowds are a reflection of the locals' immense popularity - ***affordable, dependable, accessible, and unmatched in speed and convenience.*** With some adjustments, regular commuters can travel more comfortably, even escaping the rush. Haven't we managed to do this all our lives?"

Some tips:

- **Start early, and if possible, go down:** Sacrifice some sleep at home and board an early train. You can always catch up on sleep during the journey.
- **Offer seats to seniors,** women, and individuals carrying children.
- **After sitting for about 30 minutes,** consider giving up your seat to those standing - it's a kind gesture, and prolonged sitting isn't good for health anyway.
- **Be prepared:** Arriving early ensures a comfortable seat. Use your time wisely - read newspapers, solve crossword puzzles, study, review work, or indulge in hobbies. Many women clean vegetables, and knitters do knitting. If none of this interests you, simply enjoy the evolving urban scenery outside.

And if all else fails, think of those stuck in traffic jams on roads - ***breathing in smoke continuously and surrounded by vehicles with no end in sight! In comparison, being amidst diverse faces,***

languages, and cultures in a local train seems far more appealing.

Avoid risky behavior:

- Never lean out of the train or attempt stunts . Poles don't discriminate—they can be fatal!
- Do not cross tracks - Always use overbridges.
- Avoid boarding a moving train.
- Always disembark in the same direction as the train's movement.
- If trains are delayed due to technical glitches, avoid overcrowded ones and consider alternatives.

"Locals are a microcosm of life, rich with invaluable lessons and life changing stories, creating a ***magical experience on wheels. They showcase the oneness of humanity, serving as a living testament to unity in diversity. Like a sacred Scripture in motion, they reveal the struggles for survival and the remarkable refinement of the human spirit achieved along the way. Let us honor and cherish this marvel with heartfelt gratitude and appreciation."*** Aravi said.

What Next?

As we wrap up, let's ponder - if given a chance ***at rebirth,*** what would we choose to become?

"***A motorman, steering the local train with flair.*** Just picture yourself at the helm, taking in the breathtaking view of Mumbai's ever-changing tapestry of life and railside views. There's nothing quite like it."

Muraleedharan Appath

www.ingramcontent.com/pod-product-compliance
Lightning Source LLC
LaVergne TN
LVHW041234150826
845673LV00008B/2381

* 9 7 9 8 8 9 7 4 4 4 3 4 2 *